Edward Bouverie Pusey

Christianity Without the Cross. A Corruption of the Gospel of Christ

Three Sermons Preached Before the University of Oxford

Edward Bouverie Pusey

Christianity Without the Cross. A Corruption of the Gospel of Christ
Three Sermons Preached Before the University of Oxford

ISBN/EAN: 9783337160241

Printed in Europe, USA, Canada, Australia, Japan

Cover: Foto ©Lupo / pixelio.de

More available books at **www.hansebooks.com**

CHRISTIANITY WITHOUT THE CROSS
A CORRUPTION OF THE GOSPEL OF CHRIST.

A SERMON,

PREACHED BEFORE

THE UNIVERSITY OF OXFORD,

ON SEPTUAGESIMA SUNDAY, 1875.

WITH A NOTE ON

"MODERN CHRISTIANITY A CIVILISED HEATHENISM."

BY THE

REV. E. B. PUSEY, D.D.

REGIUS PROFESSOR OF HEBREW, AND CANON OF CHRIST CHURCH.

SOLD BY
JAMES PARKER & CO., OXFORD,
AND 377, STRAND, LONDON;
AND RIVINGTONS,
LONDON, OXFORD, AND CAMBRIDGE.

1875.

CHRISTIANITY WITHOUT THE CROSS
A CORRUPTION OF THE GOSPEL OF CHRIST.

S. LUKE ix. 23.

*"And He said unto all, If any will come after Me,
let him deny himself, and take up his cross daily,
and follow Me."*

DOES then our Redeeming Lord indeed speak these
words to us? Is there no way out of them? Would
He still say them, if He were to come again upon
earth and preach in our marketplaces? But was
He not then the Eternal Word? Did He not
say, "Heaven and earth shall pass away, but My
words shall not pass away?" Does He not say,
"The word that I have spoken, the same shall
judge him in the last Day?" Does not that Other
Comforter, as He called Him, that "best Preacher,"
God the Holy Ghost, still preach those words to us
many times in the year? Are they not part of the
"everlasting Gospel[a]?"

But what then? Does not only men's practice,
in great measure, fall short of the Pattern and
Ideal set before them, but is, as has been said,
"Modern Christianity a civilised Heathenism[b]?"
Do men not only but half-believe our Blessed
Lord's words, but is His plan a failure? Have
we altogether parted with Him Whom we adore,

[a] Rev. xiv. 6.   [b] See Note at the end.

B 2

Whom we desire to love? Or, how is this state
of things around us compatible with the Divinity
of the Gospel, which He was?

Compatible it certainly is, since He predicted it.
For what else do the parables of the tares and the
wheat; the good and bad fish in the one net of the
kingdom of God; the three sorts of soil, upon which
the seed sown was wasted, and the one soil in
which it yielded varied proportions of fruit; the
wise and foolish virgins; the sheep and the goats;
the slothful servant who knew his Lord's will and
did it not; the many called and the few chosen; the
wide gate and the broad way which leadeth unto
destruction, and the many who go in thereat; those
who shall say in that Day, "Have we not pro-
phesied in Thy Name, and in Thy Name done
many wondrous works?" and to whom He shall
say "I never knew you;" those who should cause
one of those little ones who believe in Him to
offend, and for whom it would be better that they
should be cast into the sea;—What is this and
the like, but that chequered scene of good and
evil which our eyes behold? Nay, He pictures
the times before His Coming[c] as just such times
of luxury, selfishness, worldliness, as we see all
around us. He tells us of that abounding of ini-
quity and the consequent chillness of love[d], which
we too well know. One who less knew the human
heart than He Who made it, or the intensity of
its self-will, might well have thought that it could
not resist such overpowering love, as God has
shewed us. It is not in the heart of man to ima-

[c] S. Matt. xxiv. 38, 39.   [d] Ib. 12.

gine such obduration of the soul against it, even
as some picture to themselves a conversion of the
soul after death, in those who will not, to the end,
be turned back to God here. One who had not a
Divine knowledge of the heart would not have ima-
gined such Divine love wasted. To human success
it is essential to believe its own power to succeed.
" ᵉ They can because they think they can," is true
of men. Divine wisdom alone knew the limits
which self-obdurating free-will would set to the
prevailingness of Divine love and Divine grace.
Success and failure were predicted at once; Divine
success from Divine power: partial failure con-
temporaneous with the success, from the limit
which God set to the putting-forth of His own
Omnipotency—our free-will.

We may then well dispense ourselves from the
superfluous task of vindicating our Redeemer. The
love of God, revealed to us in Christ, has eternal
ends, even beyond that unutterable bliss of those
who will to be saved. "God hath set us the Apostles last," S. Paul says ᶠ, "as a spectacle to the
world and to Angels and to men ,"—" ᵍ to the intent
that now unto the principalities and powers in
heavenly places might be known through the Church
the manifold wisdom of God." "The Angels," we
are told, " ʰ desire to look into the Sufferings of
Christ and the glory which should follow." Nay,
even apart from the hints which Holy Scripture
gives us, it were inconceivable that the mystery of
the Incarnation, the union of God the Creator with

ᵉ Possunt, quia posse videntur.   ᶠ 1 Cor. iv. 9.
  ᵍ Eph. iii. 10.   ʰ 1 S. Pet. i. 12.

us, should not in ways, more unutterably vast than
we can imagine, affect every order and indivi-
dual of that creation, those gigantic Intelligences
and Powers, of whom we know scarce anything
except what is conveyed to us by their names,
but over whom, with us, our Incarnate Lord is
Head[i]. But, leaving to Almighty God the wisdom
of His own doings, it concerns us more nearly, yea
most nearly, (for it may be our salvation)—since
there is this evident contrast between the precepts
of our Lord and the outward shew of much which
thinks itself Christian, which would be shocked
and feel itself aggrieved or insulted, if it were told
that it is not Christian,—have we corrupted Christianity? The question ought not to startle us.
Where are those seven Churches, to whom God
the Holy Ghost dictated those seven Epistles in
the Apocalypse, and of the corruption of which[j],
or their chequered good and evil[k], or even of whose
unmixed good, yet of the necessity of perseverance[l],
He wrote? And yet what He said to them, He
says expressly that He said to all who have an ear
to hear, "[m] He that hath an ear to hear, let him
hear what the Spirit saith unto the Churches."
Corruptions in the Western Churches before the
reformation were miserably great; all acknowledge
it : there would not have been otherwise a rent so
great. Protestant missionaries have not much
more to say of the Eastern Church. I am not speak-

[i] Eph. i. 10, 21. Phil. ii. 10. 1 S. Pet. iii. 22.

[j] Sardis, Rev. iii. 1—6 ; Laodicea, Ib. 14—21.

[k] Ephesus, Ib. ii. 1—7 ; Pergamos, Ib. 12—17.

[l] Smyrna, ii. Ib. 8—11 ; Thyatira, Ib. 18—29 ; Philadelphia,
Ib. iii. 7—13.   [m] Ib. iii. 22.

ing of our devotions, or of that which, as a Church,
we teach and set forth as truth; but of that which
they contradict, what we should amend if we fol-
lowed them—our popular maxims, our lives. Is
our 19th century Christianity, in all which concerns
our lives, in that habitual every day course of life
whereby we are pleasing or displeasing God, our
standard of what is right or wrong, like that which
our Lord left on earth for us to follow?

Again, I speak not of the poor. They are the spe-
cial heritage of Christ. His mission was especially
to preach the Gospel unto *them.* He pronounced
them "blessed." He declared that "theirs is the
kingdom of Heaven." Even now they bear still
the likeness of His outward lot. They wear His
livery and badge. Poverty is full often a sort of
sacrament to them, conveying to them His hidden
grace; their privations, when well-endured by His
grace, are " ⁿ a kind of sacrifice to Him; they, even
by their patient endurance, will have some portion
of the reward of those who not only believe, but also
suffer for His sake." And happily they are the
largest portion of Christendom. Christ is probably
more often to be found in the hovels of the poor
than in the drawing-rooms of the rich. At the
worst I should think that in that great Babylon,
our metropolis, the atmosphere of S. Giles' was
more healthy for the fruits of the Gospel than the
air of Belgravia.

But again, I speak not of individuals. However
horribly like, not *their* condition, but our's also, is
to that of Dives, God alone knows who are really

ⁿ Keble's Lenten Sermons, p. 19.

such. In outward luxuries we far exceed him.
The whole realm of luxury and comfort has ex-
panded, even to those who have fewest of what
would be called luxuries. He had not the neces-
saries of his breakfast from the two opposite ends
of the earth, or his fuel from the earth's bowels,
gained by the unacknowledged and unthanked toils
of his fellow-men. It were well, exceeding well for
us, if we were content with the luxuries which the
Prophets condemned. This outward lot is not, we
must hope, their and our all. In one way it bears
most on our judgement hereafter, whether we are
steadily setting ourselves to act up to what we
know. We are not responsible, in the same degree,
for the fog and mist around us, which hinders our
seeing beyond a little way, unless we could ourselves
remove it. And yet, although we be swept along
by the torrent of tyrant custom, or may not see
how effectually to resist it, we must often have felt
a misgiving, "Are we honest with the words of
Christ?" Let us hear Him, as we just now heard
Him. It is He, our Redeemer, our Judge, Who
speaks, "If any will come after Me, let him deny
himself and take up his cross daily and follow Me."

Our Lord sets Himself before them to accept or
to refuse, if any will. God so loveth the free
choice and love of His creatures, that He draggeth
us not as stones, but draws us with cords of
loving-kindness. God became Man to win our love.
He calls us on no road which He hath not Himself
tracked with His Blood. The closer we follow,
(even reason tells us,) the nearer we come to Him.
He respects our freewill, in which He created us,

whether we *will* follow Him or no; but, if we
will to follow Him, the way is but one. He is the
Truth, and cannot bid us follow Him in ways
which lead away from Him. He cannot bid us
serve Him and that which is contrary to Him.
"Ye cannot serve God and Mammon." It is a
contradiction, as it would be to walk on two opposite roads at once, to go at once backwards
and forwards. The words are simple, "If any will
to follow Me, let him deny himself, and take up his
cross and follow Me." Self-renunciation stands at
the threshold of the school of Christ. Our Master
saith not, (in our petty way of speaking of "self-
denial") "let him lay aside this or that," but
"himself" (ἀρνησάσθω ἑαυτόν). It were little to renounce what one *has*, unless one renounce also
what one *is*. One might renounce anything one
has, and plume ourselves on having renounced it.
The self which we are to renounce is the self,
which is opposed to God and the will of God.
"We are," says a father[o], "one thing, as we
are fallen by sin; another, as we were created by
nature; one thing, which we *have* made, another,
which we *were* made. Let us forsake ourselves,
such as we have by sinning made ourselves, and
remain ourselves, such as by grace we have been
made. The proud, who by conversion to Christ
hath been made humble, has forsaken himself.
The luxurious, who has changed his life to conti-
nence, hath renounced what he was. The covetous,
who hath ceased to seek for gain, and hath learned
to give bountifully of his own, hath forsaken

[o] S. Greg. in Evangel. Hom. 32. n. 2 (abridged).

himself. He is himself by nature; he is not himself in ill. Paul had denied himself, who said,
'yet I live, but not I.' Dead was that fierce persecutor, and there had begun to live the pious
preacher. 'But Christ liveth in me.' 'I,' he saith,
'am dead from my former self, for I live no longer
after the flesh; but not dead essentially, for in
Christ I live spiritually.' Let then the Truth say,
'If any will to come after Me, let him deny himself;' for unless any cease from himself, he ap-
proacheth not to Him, Who is above himself; nor
can he lay hold of that which is beyond himself, if
he know not how to do to death what he is."

So far the first step of being a disciple of Christ
is to "cease to do evil," as Isaiah [p] says. But it
is not an abnegation of this or that evil thing in
him, but himself. It is not, to renounce sensuality,
and retain pride; to renounce sloth, and retain ambi-
tion; to cease to abuse God's gifts, and by self-
exaltation to be ungrateful to the Giver; to refrain
from active evil, yet to be ashamed of Christ and
His words; to diminish self-indulgence, yet shew
no mercy to the poor; to prize the truth, yet speak
evil of dignities; to own one's self a miserable
sinner, and be angry because one is slighted. Real
self-renunciation is in all things, and as one tied
by one leg may walk for miles, but quit not the
spot where he is tied; so one unrenounced evil
habit keeps the soul Satan's prisoner, that he
cannot follow Christ. Whoso renounceth not his
whole self is like one who walks all night in a

[p] Is. i. 16. "Depart from evil and do good." Ps. xxxiv. 14,
xxxvii. 27.

mist, and finds himself in the morning close to what was a burthen to him and what he had thrown down.

Self-surrender must be complete. Else it is, at best, the surrender not of self, but of one part of self; a sacrifice, like that utter destruction of what was vile and worthless in Saul's eyes, for which God rejected himself; a sacrifice, such as men will offer to any of the idols of this world, of that which costs them nothing, compared to that which they gain. All of us have renewed our vows to re- nounce the devil and—not some of his works but *all;* not some of the sinful lusts of the flesh, but *all;* to love God with *all* our heart, with *all* our mind, with *all* our soul, with *all* our strength; we have " renounced the devil and *all* his works; the vain pomp and glory of the world, and the carnal desires of the flesh, so that we will not follow nor be led by them." What can we retain, which shall not brand us as perjured persons, perjured to our Re- deemer and our God? One deadly sin, wilfully and knowingly indulged, absolutely separates from God. Not that the sinner's state is so hopeless, or that he need be so far separate from God, as by mani- fold sins, though deadly sins seldom come singly; but all seeming or real natural good unites not to God one, whom one unrepented, repeated sin separates from Him. It is God Himself Who says, " [q] If a man keep the whole law, yet offend in one point, he is guilty of all;" for all are one whole, and One is the Giver of all.

This lies at the threshold of the Gospel: one

[q] S. James ii. 10.

deadly sin, persevered in, separates from Christ; one deadly sin persevered in, enlists us in war against Christ; and makes us, instead of soldiers of Christ, mercenaries of the Enemy; our name of Christian, until we repent, brands us as deserters.

But our Lord goes on, " let him deny himself, and take up his cross." " Here," some may tell me, " we have a metaphor, and metaphors may not have a very precise meaning." Doubtless, many of us have passed over this saying, as not having a very definite meaning. Yes! but also metaphors may have a very deep meaning; nay, it is for the sake of that deeper meaning, that the metaphor is used at all, because it expresses more than could be taught in plain terms, without it. And here the metaphor is from Christ Himself, and the bitter Passion which He willingly underwent for love of each one of us.

It was probably the first time that our Blessed Lord had spoken plainly of that Death. He had before told them of the mourning, when He, Whom S. John Baptist had spoken of as the Bridegroom, [r]should be taken from them: He had declared their future blessedness, " [s]when men shall hate you, and shall cast out your name as evil for the Son of Man's sake." Now, that S. Peter had, in the name of all, confessed," Thou art the Christ of God," He told them (it seems for the first time) plainly; "[t] The Son of Man must suffer many things, and be rejected of the elders and chief priests and scribes, and be slain and be raised the third day." And

---

[r] S. Luke v. 35, S. Mark ii. 20, S. Matt. ix. 15.

[s] S. Luke vi. 22.   [t] Ib. ix. 22.

when Peter had deprecated this, and received that severe rebuke, as doing the part of the Evil one, and "ᵘsavouring not the things that be of God, but the things that be of men," then, lest we should think that He said this to Apostles only, "ᵛHe called *the people* with His disciples," and said to them. this about the cross, and added that aweful sanction, "ʷWhat shall it profit a man, if he shall gain the whole world, and lose his own soul? or what shall a man give in exchange for his soul?" and then, "Whoso shall be ashamed of Me and of My words in this sinful and adulterous generation, of him also shall the Son of Man be ashamed, when He cometh in the glory of the Father and of the holy Angels." O the horrible woe of him, from whom Christ, our only hope, shall turn away His Face in that Day!

Is there then no escape from it? Did our Lord, the Truth, mean what He said? Let me ask you an opposite question. Did our Lord, being God, become Man, only that His disciples should lead as easy lives as they can, multiply to themselves as many comforts and luxuries as they can, say to our souls, with the rich man whose soul was that night demanded of him to give account of his stewardship, "ˣSoul, take thine ease, eat, drink and be merry," so only that thou be not drunken? Is His law, "Thou canst not serve God and mammon," obsolete? Or is what He declared impossible, become possible with time? Are we to turn our Lord's Woes into Blesseds and His Blesseds into

ᵘ S. Mark viii. 32, 33.   ᵛ Ib. 34.
ʷ Ib. 36-38.   ˣ S. Luke xxii. 19.

Woes, and still call ourselves His disciples ? Shall
we say," ʸ Blessed are ye that are rich :" " Blessed
are ye that are full :" and, " Woe unto you that are
poor : " " woe unto you that hunger now." It is
what men's every day lives, what our boast that
" we English understand our comforts," what our
self-gratulations seem to say. Can we persuade
ourselves that our treasure is *not*, where our heart
is ? or that our heart is not *there*, for which we
toil. A heathen said, " The despot money commands or serves each ᶻ." It commands those who
slave for it. We are not less its slaves, if we toil
for it, to spend on ourselves, our comforts and our
luxuries.

If we cannot find one word of our Lord's to
excuse our living for this world, and hoping to
gain heaven, how did they understand Him, to
whom He spake or revealed Himself ? Let us ask
him, men's favourite Apostle, because, while he
teaches that we are " justified by faith," they hide
from themselves, that he speaks not of an inactive
faith but of a "faith that worketh by love." What
didst thou, Paul, understand by this metaphor,
which men satisfy themselves with calling a metaphor because they do not like its meaning ? What
didst thou understand by this doctrine of the
cross, thou who dost tell us, that thou didst " de-
termine ᵃ to know nothing but Jesus Christ, and
Him crucified ?" Didst thou live to the world or
to Him Who died for thee ? " God forbid," he

ʸ S. Luke vii. 20, 21, 24, 25.
ᶻ Imperat aut servit regina pecunia cuique.
ᵃ 1 Cor. ii. 2.

says[b], "that I should glory save in the cross of our Lord Jesus Christ, whereby the world is crucified to me, and I unto the world." In the cross of Christ the world was crucified to him and was dead; it had no power over him to hold him, for it was dead: it had no attractions for him, no winningness to him, for to him it was a corpse. And he too was crucified to the world on that same cross. He could, like his Lord, embrace the world with outstretched arms, in that large heart, but not with any longing for it, save to win it to his Lord. He was "co-crucified (συνεσταύρωμαι) with Christ," and had no will, no longing, no affections, no love for it, but Christ's: he heard not its revilings; he heeded not its praises; for he was dead to it. "[c]All which it loved was a cross unto him, the delights of the flesh, honours, riches, vain praises of men: all which it counted a cross, to *that* he clave, to *that* he was nailed: *that* he embraced with his whole heart." His former self was dead. "I have been and am crucified with Christ; it is no longer I that live but Christ liveth in me." He was dead to all besides; he felt them not, heeded them not, cared not for them, any more than one dead; all of himself was dead and gone; his human passions were nailed to the cross of Christ, and were dead; "dead," says a father[d], "were pleasure and pain and wrath and fear and timidity and vehement emotion and pride and rashness, and memory of injuries, and envy and self-

[b] Gal. vi. 14.

[c] S. Bern. de Quadr. Serm. vii. n. 1. Opp. i. 833.

[d] S. Greg. Nyss. in Cant. Hom. xv. Tom. i. p. 695.

defence, and covetousness or any other affection which defiles the soul—He had stripped off all which was not in Christ, and his life was Christ, Who was Sanctification and Purity and Immortality and Light and Truth." "Not I live, but Christ liveth in me." Christ wrought all his works in him; Christ spake by his tongue, so that he spake those fiery words of persuasive burning love; Christ was the Heart of that vast heart which embraced all, Jew and heathen, those who were won, and those who could be won, and those who could not yet be won, by and to the love of Christ, breathing forth the fire of Divine love, with which he was himself kindled. Christ in him made known in all the world the riches of the mystery of the faith in Him; Christ filled up in His servant "'what was yet lacking of His own Sufferings for His Body's sake, which is the Church;" those sufferings which He willed should be endured in His members for His members, that so His own meritorious Sufferings might reach unto all those for whom He died. "To him to live was Christ." Christ was the source of his spiritual life; Christ was, within him, the perpetual maintainer of his life; Christ was the Pattern and Exemplar of his life; Christ was the end and object and substance of his life; Christ was in all things the mainspring of his life, the informer of his words, the inworker of his acts, the endurer of his sufferings, the instrengthener against temptation by His grace and gracious Presence; in Whom he strove according to *His* working, Who worked in him

' Col. i. 25.

in might Divine. And so, since Christ lived in him and to him to live was Christ, "to die was gain;" for the persecutor's sword was the finisher of his toils, yielding him up to Him, for Whom and in Whom and by Whom he lived.

Does this life, this death, belong to Paul alone? What saith he to those whom he had won to Christ? "ᶠIn Christ Jesus I have begotten you through the Gospel; wherefore, I beseech you, be ye imitators of me." "Be ye," *he* says who was crucified with Christ, "ᵍbe ye imitators of me, as I also of Christ." Nay, he says of those new converts to the faith, "ʰye also became imitators of us and of the Lord." How? In our Lord's exceptional presence at the marriage feast, or in eating with publicans and sinners? Perhaps in this too, if so they might win them to Christ; but what is recorded is, that they received the word "in much affliction, with joy in the Holy Ghost." As the Apostles departed from the presence of the Council, rejoicing that they were counted worthy to suffer shame for His Nameⁱ, so to these, things grievous became joyous; grievous to the bodily frame, with spiritual joy, "joy in the Holy Ghost." Yet these were no exceptional Christians; "model Christians" only in that they were models for others to follow, in that from "them the word sounded out to others." Yet these had been converts, converts from the ordinary heathen vices. "Ye turned to God from idols to serve the living and true God." How? Amid self-indulgence, the pomps and vani-

---

ᶠ 1 Cor. iv. 15, 16.   ᵍ Ib. xi. 1.   ʰ 1 Thess. i. 6.
ⁱ Acts v. 14.

ties of the world? No, but with one longing expectation to see Him, to Whom they owed their all, to wait the return of Him Who was crucified for them, Whose cross they, like Simon of Cyrene, bare after Him. "To wait for His Son from heaven, Whom He raised from the dead, Jesus which delivered us from the wrath to come."

This was the common lot of Christians then. "[j] Ye became imitators of the Churches of God, which in Judea are in Christ Jesus." Wherein? That they suffered. "*For*," he adds, "ye have suffered like things of your countrymen, even as they have of the Jews." As he says to another Church; "[k] To you it is given not only to believe in Him, but also"—What is this gift, this grant bestowed by God's love upon them? How should we fill this up? The last thing, I fear, with which we should fill it up, would be that which he adds, "but also to suffer with Him."

But these, you may say, were days of persecution, from which, by God's mercy, we are exempt. It is, I trust, "in God's mercy." For look at any picture of post-Apostolic times, in which Christians were again braced up by one of the ten persecutions; they who were such as we mostly are, in ease or worldliness or self-indulgence, apostatised. And apostacy involved the formal renunciation and blaspheming of Christ, Who died for us. But the most commonplace Christian life was not, S. Paul says, without crucifixion. All was "with Christ;" all, past and future. With Him we hope to live for ever, but not otherwise than if we first

[j] 1 Thess. ii. 14.　　　　　　[k] Phil. i. 29.

die and remain dead with Him. "If we be dead with Christ, we believe that we shall also live with Him." In S. Paul's language[l], we "co-died," "were co-crucified, were co-interred, were co-implanted in His death;" with Him, "God co-crucified" co-raised us," "co-seated us in heavenly places with Him." Are we to be joined with Christ in everything which is not of us or by us, and only not with Christ in that which is our own, which it is in our power to give or to refuse? Not so. S. Paul says, "[m]It is a faithful saying, 'If we co-die, we shall also co-live: if we endure, we shall also co-reign." We have heard what crucifixion was to S. Paul, a living death, death to himself, and life in Christ. Think you that he would use the image of some easy painless process? Would *you?* Could you gravely say to one another, that you were crucified to anything? Yet S. Paul, having arrayed over against each other the two opposed armies, the works of the flesh and the works of the Spirit, sums up— "[n] They that are Christ's have crucified the flesh with the affections and lusts." Granted that by the flesh the Apostle means the ill deeds of the flesh, yet see the completeness of the death in which they are held. Not one ill-deed, but all; not one disposition to sin, but all; not one concupiscence, but all; nailed, motionless, powerless to the cross of Christ. "We *then,*" says a father[o], "crucify the

---

[l] Rom. vi. 4, 5, 6. viii. 17, Gal. ii. 20. Eph. ii. 5, 6, Col. ii. 12, 13, iii. 1, 2 Tim. ii. 11. See Dr. Pusey's Scriptural Doctrine of Holy Baptism p. 171.   [m] 2 Tim. ii. 11, 12.   [n] Gal. v. 24.

[o] S. Greg. in Job c. 8. L. viii. c. xliv. n. 73. Opp. i. 277. He begins, "Contrariwise, it is well said of the elect by Paul "They that are Christ's &c."

flesh with the affections and lusts, if we in such
wise restrain appetite, as therewith to seek nothing
from the glory of the world. For he who macerates
his body but pants after honours, crucifies the
flesh ; but by concupiscence he lives to the world
yet more, because, often through a phantom of
holiness, he, being unworthy, gains some place of
rule, whereto he would attain by no labour, unless
he had some show of virtue."

Is this the glowing language of S. Paul only ? Is
it only *his* language, to whom on his wonderful
conversion, which we are to commemorate to-
morrow, Christ Himself shewed how great things
he must suffer for His Name's sake ?   Is it only a
transcript of *his* life who was "in labours more
abundant, in deaths oft ? "   Will any other Apostle
of our Master, Who was crucified for us, give us
easier terms ?

You would scarce expect it of him, our Lord's
brother, whose knees were hardened like a camel's,
being bent evermore in prayer to God for forgive-
ness for his people[p].   Certainly *his* idea of the
"summum bonum" is different from that of Heathen philosophy, nor could it ever occur to any
one apart from Christ and His Cross.   It would
not occur to us, *now* living in the midst of, and
boasting ourselves of the Gospel of Christ.   "[q] My
brethren, count it all joy," the sum of joy, com-
prising in itself all other joys, "when ye fall into
divers trials."   And these were no passing trials,

---

[p] Hegesippus in Eusebius (H. E. ii. 23.) who says that Heg.
related most accurately the history of S. James.

[q] S. Jas. i. 2.

but enduring. For their benefit was endurance.
They were to test endurance to the utmost, and
yield the soul perfected for "'the crown of life,"
which the Lord hath promised to them that love
Him. The joy of S. James is the exultation of
S. Paul; "ᵉyea, we glory in tribulations," and
on the self-same ground, that the Christian's joy
cometh from being perfected by the Cross. "Tribulation worketh patience, and patience experience,
and experience hope, and hope maketh not ashamed." For both Apostles repeated their Master's
lesson, "ᵗBlessed are they that mourn; for they shall
be comforted;" "Blessed are they which are persecuted for righteousness sake; for theirs is the
kingdom of heaven." Whence the Martyr's cry
so often was "ᵘThanks be to God."

But what of the opposite condition which men
now count so happy? "The rich man," he saysᵛ,
"exulteth in that wherein is humiliation." He assumes it as a thing known or which ought to be
known to them: "Friendship with the world is
enmity with God;" "Whoso would be the friend
of the world is madeʷ" by the very fact, by being
so minded, (καθίσταται) "an enemy of God." He
that loveth the one, as our Lord saith, despiseth
the other. Such are already "adulterous souls,"
fallen away from God Who hath made them His
own, and giving themselves over to His enemy.

ʳ Ib. i. 12.   ˢ Rom. v. 3.   ᵗ S. Matt. v. 4—6.
ᵘ "The Christian being condemned giveth thanks." Tertull.
Apol. c. 1. p. 4, Oxf. Tr. and note m. and Ruinart, Acta Mart.
ᵛ S. James i. 10, supplying καυχᾶται as in Phil. iii. 19, "whose
glory is in their shame." Alford.   ʷ S. Jas. iv. 4.

Or ask S. Peter, him who would have dissuaded
his Master from the Cross, him, who was drawn
by love of his Master to the judgement-hall, and
there cowered before a little maid and denied Him,
to whom, our Lord, foresignifying his death, said,
" Follow thou Me." Wherein did he understand
that following to be? For our Lord says to *us*,
as to him, "Follow Me." "ˣIf when ye do well
and suffer, ye take it patiently, this is acceptable
with God; for even thereunto were ye called."—
called whereto? to "suffer patiently for well doing."
Suffering he declares to be the very object of
our calling, even as S. Paul and Barnabas " con-
firmed the souls of the disciples in every city" where
they had preached, telling them that "ʸwe must
through much tribulation enter into the kingdom
of God." But S. Peter assigns, further, the ground
of our being so called, because we are members of
a thorn-crowned Head; " *because* Christ also suffered for us, leaving us a copy," (ὑπογραμμὸν) as
children copy line by line and stroke by stroke,
that we should follow close upon His steps, marking
them, placing our feet as nearly as we can to them;
and those steps were, in that sad road to Calvary,
tracked in His own Blood, shed for us.

Again, see how close he brings us to our Lord.
"ᶻChrist then having suffered in the flesh," (as
he had said, " Christ died for our sins, the Just
for the unjust" to bring us to God,) "arm yourselves likewise with the same mind"—"arm yourselves," not assuredly for a listless peace; "with
the same mind as Christ" when He suffered; "for

ˣ 1 S. Pet. ii. 20.   ʸ Acts xiv. 22.   ᶻ 1 S. Pet. iv. 1, 2.

he that hath suffered in the flesh hath ceased from sin." We, being members of Christ, are counted as having ourselves suffered with Christ, " that we should no longer live the rest of our life to the lust of men, but to the will of God;" that the one object of our lives, our affections, our new regenerate being, should be the will of God. The thought of Christ crucified, the sharing of His sufferings, not without us only, but within us, is the panoply of Christians. Or look at that saying, "If the righteous scarcely (with difficulty) be saved," and that, in view of judgement through which he has to pass and to be sifted therein. Surely this does not speak of an easy, good-natured, effortless life, but a life passed, as he also says,· "[a] If ye call upon Him as Father, Who without respect of persons judgeth every man's work, pass the time of your sojourning here with fear," and that the more, he adds, on account of the exceeding preciousness of the price of our redemption, the precious Blood of Christ. We have to give account, not of our lives only, but of the terrible ingratitude of despising our Redeemer.

Once more, let us ask him, the beloved disciple, the Apostle of love, who lay on his Master's breast and drank there the streams of wisdom and of love, he who speaks so much of the love of God towards us; of the propitiation for our sins; of the life in God begun in us; of the beatific vision of God. What saith he? "[b] He that saith that he abideth in Him ought himself also to walk even as He

[a] Ib. i. 17.   [b] 1 S. John ii. 6.

walked." " [c] If any man love the world, the love of
the Father is not in him." " Abide in Me," Jesus
says, "and I in you." "Abide in Me," of Whom ye
have been made members, by faith and love and
obedience, and I will abide in you by My grace,
and the continual influx of My Spirit. If then we
abide in Him, we are to walk as He walked. We
all have an idea that we are to keep, in a general
way, God's commandments, not to swear, not to
lie, not to commit certain excesses. But does this
suffice, to walk as Christ walked? Is this mere
negative or limited Christianity to walk as *He*,
Whom we own as our Exemplar, walked? " What,"
says an approved writer[d], "is to walk as He walked,
but to despise all prosperous things, which He
despised; to fear nothing adverse which He bare;
to do cheerfully what He did; to teach to do what
He commanded; to hope what He promised; to
follow where He went before; to bestow benefits
on the ungrateful also; not to requite ill-wishers
as they deserve; to pray for enemies, to love the
good, to pity the perverse, to invite those averted
(from God), to receive lovingly those converted;
to endure patiently the treacherous and the proud;
to die to one's own sins as He for our's; for as
one dead in the body detracts from none, injures
none, despises none, corrupts, envies, flatters, courts
none, so they who have crucified their flesh with
the affections and lusts, living to God, live not to
these or the like sins." "What must he do," says

[c] 1 S. John ii. 15.

[d] Pomerius de vit. contempl. ii. 21. (in S. Prosper Opp. T. ii.)
abridged.

a father [c], " to whom the great name of Christian
has been vouchsafed ? What else than diligently
judge in himself thoughts, words, deeds, whether
each of these look to Christ or are alien from
Him ?"

You would not expect relaxation from S. Jude,
whose whole Epistle is one upbraiding of the sins
of false teachers and relapsers. But among their
very heavy sins, it is startling to our self-indulgent
age, to find the habit of our times, "[f] feeding themselves without fear." He does not mention glut-
tony or excess in meat or wine, but that, in supplying the wants of nature, they fed without
reverence and awe, lest they should do amiss.

So did the goodly company of the Apostles
inculcate with one voice, a life to be led above the
world, contrary to the world and conformed to
our Redeemer, as *the* way of salvation.

We have been in the habit of speaking dispa-
ragingly of a former generation, which spoke much
of our Lord as our Example; we thought it cold; we
thought much of our revived preaching of the Cross
and of the Crucified. I fear, that much of the religion of the present day has been rather the belief
of a doctrine, a revelation, than a personal belief
in Him our Redeemer ; that believing, so far truly,
our redemption, many have forgotten Him as an
Example. Could we take up with such poor mea-
sures of attainment, if we seriously thought of Him
as the likeness which we were to copy, which was,
by His Spirit, to be formed in us ? Look at them

[c] S. Greg. Nyss. de perf. Christiani forma. Opp. iii. 296.

[f] S. Jude 12.

one by one. We might think perhaps, that we
had something of meekness or gentleness, or charity,
or peaceableness ; or, more probably, that we were
not flagrantly the very opposite; but meekness
of Christ, long-suffering of Christ, lowliness of
Christ, gentleness of Christ, self-sacrificing love of
Christ, self-consuming zeal of Christ, burning
thirst of Christ for saving souls, hunger of Christ
to do His Father's will, unwearied tenderness of
Christ,—we see you in His wearisome life on earth,
but where are those, who set themselves, in the
full endeavour of their souls, to copy these in themselves ?

Are men really disciples of Christ, or of some
phantom Christ? Him, God-Man, Who was crucified for them, or a mythical Christ, the creature of
their own imaginings? Christ, to Whose likeness
they are to be conformed, or a Christ, such an one
as themselves, formed in their own image ? " One
stood before S. Martin, (S. Martin himself related
itᵍ) enveloped in a glittering radiance, clad in royal
robes, crowned with a golden and jewelled diadem,
with face serene and bright looks, and said to him,
" I am Christ. I am now descending upon earth,
and I willed first to manifest myself to thee. Acknowledge me whom thou seest, I am Christ."
Martin at first gazed at him in silence : then,
taught by God, answered, " Jesus, the Lord, an-
nounced not, that He should come in glittering
clothing and radiant with a diadem. I will not
believe that Christ is come, save in that state and
form in which He suffered, save with the shew of

ᵍ Life of S. Martin c. 25, in Church of the Fathers, c. 21. fin.

the Wounds of the Cross." Forthwith the Evil one
(for it was he) vanished. "Many spirits are
abroad, more are issuing from the pit," says the
relater [h]; "the credentials which they display are
the precious gifts of mind, beauty, richness, depth,
originality. Christian, look hard at them with
Martin in silence, and then ask for the print of the
nails."

> "[i] Smooth open ways, good store;
> A creed for every time and age,
> By Mammon's touch new moulded o'er and o'er,
> No cross, no war to wage;"—

Are these the prints of the nails? Is this the Creed
in the Crucified?

Shall we say to our Lord when He comes down
to be our Judge, when we shall behold *Him*, Whom
we, by our sins, have pierced? "True! Lord, I
denied myself nothing for Thee; the times were
changed and I could not but change with them; I
ate and drank, for Thou too didst eat and drink
with the publicans and sinners; I did not give to the
poor; but I paid what I was compelled to the poor-
rate, of the height of which I complained; I did
not take in little children in Thy Name, but they
were provided for; they were sent, severed indeed
from father or mother, to the poor-house, to be
taught or no about Thee, as might be; I did not
feed Thee when hungry; political economy forbade
it; but I increased the labour-market with the
manufacture of my luxuries; I did not visit Thee
when sick, but the parish doctor looked in on his

[h] J. H. Newman Ib. p. 414. fin. ed. 1836.
[i] John Keble, Lyra Apostolica no. xcviii. Dissent p. 121.

ill-paid rounds ; I did not clothe Thee when naked;
I could not afford it, the rates were so high, but
there was the workhouse for Thee to go to ; I did
not take Thee in as a stranger: but it was provided
that Thou mightest go to the 'casual-ward [k].' Had
I known that it was Thou "—"[1] And He shall say,
Forasmuch as thou didst it not to one of the least
of these, thou didst it not to Me."

Many of you, my sons, are provided with super-
fluities. You have not to stint yourselves as to
the pleasures of your age. Day by day, I suppose,
passes with all conveniences of life, or amusement
or some self-indulgences, which though not directly

[k] I said this, not of Oxford nor of any particular place, but of
the system. The poor-law, nearly 40 years ago, was reduced
into a sort of police-system, on the principle "if a man will not
work, neither let him eat." It might have been, and the writer
hoped that it would have been, supplemented by Christian charity. (See Pusey's Parochial Sermons Vol. III. p. 143. "The
Value and Sacredness of Suffering," published in 1841.) As it
is, reliance on the Poor-law interferes with Christian charity,
offers, in large towns, a mode of relief which the better poor
would starve rather than accept; and in times of suffering, as of
an epidemic, offers relief in a way which degrades the poor in
their own eyes, and of their compeers, if they accept it. What
else than a police-law is it, to separate husband and wife from
each other and from their children? If the poor, like the lower
animals, needed only food and warmth, the poor-house system
provides these, I doubt not. But the poor have souls, and loving
hearts, more loving than many rich, and to separate those whom
God has joined, as the condition of supplying them with necessa-
ries, is un-Christian and anti-Christian. "I would not be sepa-
rated from my old missus," was the remark of an aged peasant,
at the time of the change in the law, which many an aching heart
has repeated since. I fear that, in the great Day, many even
kindly people will find that reliance on the Poor-law has steeled
their heart against Christ.   [1] S. Matt. xxv. 45.

sinful are rather injurious. If our Lord was to come now, in how many do you think that you could tell Him that you had fed Him, clothed Him, supplied Him when sick? Some, I fear, could not say, that they had bestowed as much on Christ, as upon their dogs.

But if, to be saved, we must be disciples of our crucified Redeemer; and if, to be His disciples, we must imitate Him and take up our cross daily; and if, of those whom we see around us, the great mass seems to think of nothing less that taking up any cross, nay rather boast that they have no cross to bear; who, except the poor, on whom the cross is, any how, laid, "who then shall be saved?" "O Lord, Thou knowest!" "The Judge of all the Earth will do right!" God mercifully lays on the cross, in ways which we know not. Others, it may be, building on the True and Only Foundation, which is Jesus Christ, may be building thereon wood, hay, stubble, which shall be burned up, S. Paul tells, in the fire of the great Day, but themselves be saved, yet so as by fire[m]." Be not curious about others, but in God's longsuffering save thou thyself. Look up to Him the Good Shepherd Who laid down His life for the sheep, and pray Him with His pierced Hands to loose the thorns which hold thee, and to lay thee upon His shoulders: yea He will carry thee in His bosom.

Ye would not be unlike Him, Who loved you and gave Himself for you; you would not, now at least, that it has been set before you, however little you

[m] See Pusey's Lenten Sermons. Serm. v. "The losses of the saved" pp. 89—106.

may have before thought of even venturing to imitate Him. Yet such is your calling. "ⁿChristianity
is the imitation of God;" conformity to God made
Man, to Whom you have been conformed; with
Whom you have been made one; your oneness
with Whom has been so often renewed; for in the
Holy Communion (as is so often repeated to you)
if we partake worthily, "we dwell in Christ, and
Christ in us: we are one with Christ, and Christ
with us."

Any self-denial, however simple, done for love
of your Redeemer, is accepted by Him as a bearing
of His Cross. Self-denials which you, many of you,
exercise for a corruptible crown, might set you in
the way, at least, not to lose the incorruptible.
Fulness of bread which "bankereth out the wits,"
dulls also the affections towards God and man.
He, to whom Jesus manifested Himself on the way,
to whom by a wondrous miracle He had revealed
Himself; He, the chosen vessel, the teacher of the
nations; whose love suffering only kindled; "in labours more abundant, in stripes above measure, in
deaths oft;" who rejoiced to be "the off-scourings of
the world and to die daily," so that he might win
any to Christ; to whom daily sufferings were more
than his daily bread, "the marks of the Lord Jesus"
on his waled body, but who was thereby "a spectacle to the world, to angels and to men," how did
he fight, how did he win his crown? "I run," he
answers youᵒ, "not as uncertainly," without any
definite object, "so fight I, not as striking the

ⁿ S. Greg. Nyss. de Profess. Christiana. Opp. iii. 271.
ᵒ 1 Cor. ix. 26.

air; but I bring under (maltreat) my body and
bring it into subjection." To what end? to be
abundantly rewarded for his abundant sufferings?
No, but, "lest when I have preached to others—
filled the whole world with the preaching of Christ
and won to Him countless souls, "I myself should
be a castaway." If Paul, being what he was, so
feared, what shall we say? Are we wiser than
S. Paul, or have we ceased to be disciples of Him,
Who foretold, that "when the Bridegroom," Himself, shall be taken away, "then shall My disciples
fast in those days;" Who instructs us how to fast,
as well as how to pray and to give alms[p]? Are we
(it is a terrible thing to say, but this is what it
comes to) are we wiser than Christ?

We are to-day at the vestibule of those days
wherein, bearing the cross of this yearly abstinence,
we are, if we are His disciples, to follow Him Who
for our sakes did fast forty days and forty nights,
that so " by continual mortifying our corrupt affections we may be buried with Him; and through
His Cross and Passion may be brought to the
glory of His Resurrection."

Three weeks hence, you will plead that fasting
to Him Who for our sakes did fast forty days and
forty nights, and pray Him that after His likeness
you too "may use such abstinence, that your flesh
being subdued to the spirit, you may ever obey
His godly motions in righteousness and true holiness." Let not your prayers be a witness against
you.

He does not put hard things upon you. He

[p] S. Matt. vi. 16.

Who accepts the cup of cold water will accept petty self-denials. Self-indulgence is a hard master, not Jesus. Vice wears the body, self-denial braces it. Sin is an exacting tyrant, the service of God is perfect freedom.

Give yourselves anew to Him, Who gave Himself for you. He grudged not for you one drop of His Heart's Blood: grudge not to Him the price of His Blood, yourselves. Think of that place around the eternal Throne, which He by that Blood has prepared individually for you. Jesus will impart to your petty cross some of the virtue of His Saving Cross. He will make any hardness sweet to you, Who is Himself all sweetness and every pleasurable delight. He will give you His own love and

" The heart that loveth knoweth well,
What Jesus 'tis to love."

NOTE.

On " Modern Christianity a civilised Heathenism."

THE allusion to the little book "Modern Christianity a civilised Heathenism" at the beginning of my sermon, perhaps requires some explanation. I alluded to it, because I was told the minds of some were disturbed by it, not in a healthy way (which the writer intended and it might have done and, I hope, will do with others) to set them looking whether they had not been making, in different degrees, a compromise with the world or worldliness, but, according to the form of the fiction, whether, I suppose, real civilisation and real Christianity were opposed to one another; whether a Christian must become "[1] the greatest nuisance to meet," "must make an ass of himself, make himself ridiculous in the eyes of worldly people—in the opinion of modern society—every time he speaks or acts," and "be hated and laughed at for his eccentricities."

Some perhaps have been led to the terrible question, "Is Christianity a failure?" Any how, "does it bear evidence in itself, as it exists now, that it is Divine?"

The writer is, I fear, in some degree responsible for raising this question, by the form in which he has cast his book, the subject of which is the unpersuasiveness or positive offensiveness of the life of worldly persons and especially of worldly Clergy. For had he adopted a title, which would have expressed his meaning more exactly, ' *Much* modern Christianity ; "—or " Fashionable Christi-

[1] pp. 118, 119, 73.

D

anity," or "The Christianity of the worldly," or "of the wealthy" or "of the great"— "a civilised Heathenism," he would have avoided raising those other questions, and his book would only have been an application of our Blessed Lord's warning, "How hardly shall they that are rich enter into the kingdom of heaven."

For, of course, "fashionable Christianity" is but an infinitesimal portion even of "Modern Christianity." "Fashionable Christianity" may be, and too much of it, alas! I fear is, utterly false and hollow, and yet its false-ness and hollowness has nothing to do with the truth of Christianity, to which it is a contradiction and which condemns it. It is a practical corruption of Christian-ity, which civilly sets aside the teaching of the Gospel, not openly opposing it, treating our Lord's words with irreverent courtesy (as it would treat its fellow men's), yet, none the less, emptying them of their meaning. Nega-tively, as far as the lives of its adherents are conspicuous, it involves the loss of that evidence which Christians would, if they acted up to the Gospel, silently, unconsciously, but unmistakeably give, and which, the early Christians did give to the heathen, among whom their lot was cast, that "[2] the Gospel is a power of God unto salvation." When our missionaries in the neighbourhood of Tinnevelly sepa-rated their converts from their heathen countrymen, their countrymen saw, in the difference of their lives, that there was something superhuman in Christianity and asked to be taught it. Report says that the Japanese Embassadors came to England, with the thought that it might be well to introduce Christianity among the Japanese, and that, seeing what they did see on the surface, they were deterred from it. Whether there be any foundation for this or no, it is only what one should expect, if they had. We have our idols as well as they; we have, too often, a god, who is not the true God, as well as they. Mammon is not the less worshipped, because his image is not visibly set up

[2] Rom. i. 16.

in his temples; the god of this world is not less people's god, because his worship is in the heart; the idolatry is not the less real, because it is the hidden mainspring of men's acts; its icy touch is not the less felt, because it is unseen. Mammon has his servants, God has His. But unhappily, the service of Mammon is open; the service of God is for the most part out of sight; and one cannot but think, that the sight of our metropolis would give but an unfavourable impression of the power of Christianity over the hearts of men.

God Himself does oftentimes and in many ways speak to the souls of those who know Him not, but argument in proof that the Gospel is a revelation from God will have little effect in converting unbelievers, unless they see, in some way, the fruits of the Gospel in a life above nature. A religion above nature ought to produce a life above nature. Divine grace, which our Lord promises to those who are His, is supernatural: every action of grace on the soul is a miracle; the conversion of one dead in sin is a greater miracle than the raising of one physically dead: whence also our Lord said to His Apostles, "[3] He that believeth on Me, shall do greater things than these." But the lives, which what is called "the world" lives, have too often the appearance of being sweet, amiable, kindly, natural lives: yet not lives (if men are married) remarkably above nature, not apparently the lives of those whose "[4] citizenship is in heaven."

But the superficial only will judge from the surface. When the historian Niebuhr was asked in 1827 about the state of the German universities and especially of Bonn where he resided, he said to the effect; "You must not judge from what you see; you will see students lounging about in the market-place with their long pipes and their dogs; the students who are in their upper rooms at their work (which he said, were two thirds) you do not see." Much more in Christianity, which is an inward power of

[3] S. John xiv. 12.   [4] Phil. iii. 20.

God! The outward acts must, unless a person be called to a higher life, be, to the outward eye, much the same; the soul of the acts, whether what is done is done to the glory of God, or for self-exaltation, or for some secular end, is, except on long experience or from some accidental gleam of the inner self, unseen except by God. "The good housemaid," Nicole says, "sweeps the room, and prays: the good watchmaker makes watches, and prays:" and so on. Outwardly they would be doing the same acts; the difference would be seen in the long run, by the conscientiousness, with which they did them. The street-sweeper, who, while he swept his crossing, was thinking of the golden streets of the heavenly Jerusalem, would, outwardly, only sweep it more carefully. The slaves whom S. Paul exhorted, "[5] obey your masters according to the flesh with fear and trembling, with singleness of heart, as unto Christ, not with eye-service as men-pleasers, but as the servants of Christ, doing the will of God from the heart,—with good will doing service as unto the Lord and not to men," doubtless did the same outward acts, the inward motive was discoverable only by those who looked carefully; others would say of such, "[6] he is a good man, only he is a Christian."

Perhaps the subject may also be somewhat confused by the absence of any statement, what is "civilisation." Not the condition of civilised nations in general; not their objects, or pursuits; it is nothing outward; it is not literature, nor philosophy, not the perfection of mechanical arts, nor the multiplication of luxuries or comforts. We have no poet to surpass Homer; yet his age was a very simple one: "mechanical arts and merchandise flourish," Bacon tells us, "in the decay of a nation:" if luxuries were its "summum bonum," Sybaris would be without a rival, and Apicius its ideal: we have not yet discovered by what mechanical art the enormous monoliths of Thebes were removed from the quarries of Syene; it used to be a ques-

[5] Eph. vi. 5-7.   [6] Tert. Apol. c. 3, p. 8. Oxf. Tr.

tion how our ancestors could raise Stonehenge. Abstracting ourselves for a time from the actual condition of civilised nations, we should not doubt that "civilisation" means that which makes us men civilised. We learnt in our grammars the heathen notion of it, that it was "[7] ingenuas didicisse fideliter artes," in which, great emphasis must be laid upon the "fideliter," for it was a contemporary of the poet who would have fed his lampreys with the slave who broke a crystal vessel. The young slave only asked Augustus for some other death. The master's punishment for the intended murder was only to have his crystals broken and his fishpond filled up[8]. "Manners maketh man" may, I suppose, represent our modern idea of it; only that "manners" must be taken in a broad and deep meaning, including the whole relation and intercourse of man with man. Improved medical science does not authoritatively discountenance the savagery of vivisection, and this as perpetrated even by women-dissectors.

But in this sense civilisation will only be an outward aspect of Christianity; it cannot be opposed to it[9]. Any peasant, who cannot read, will, if he be indeed a Christian, be distinguished by courtesy, gentleness, refinement of feeling and manners, even tone of voice, from one who is not a Christian. Refined manners *may* be a mere outside; the manners of the world may be soulless, like the beauty of a corpse, "ere the first day of death is fled;" with "its mild angelic air, the rapture of repose that's there." The beauty may not last; but it is the beauty, left by the departed soul. But the beauty of the "manners of the world" is, in its basis, Christian. Let any one in his mind go over its instances, I think, he may see in them the Apostle's rule; "[1] in honour preferring one

---

[7] Seneca de ira iii. 40.

[8] I would venture to recommend the writer who holds British civilisation to be as corrupt as the heathen to read Döllinger Heidenthum und Judenthum.

[9] "If Christianity has any thing to do with Christ, Civilisation must ever be its deadliest foe." p. 69.　　　　　　　　　　　　　[1] Rom. xii. 10.

another;" "[2] follow after—love, patience, meekness;" "[3] the servant of the Lord must not strive, but be gentle unto all, patient;" "put them in mind to speak evil of no man, shewing *all* meekness to all men." It used to strike me, in young days, how the preference of others to self, the great shock which it evidently was to give pain to any one, the consideration of every one's feelings, the thinking of others rather than one's-self, the pains that no one should feel neglected, the deference shewn to the weak or the aged, the unconscious courtesy to those secularly inferior, were the beauty of the refined worldly manners of the "old school;" that it was acting upon Christian principle, and that if in any case it became soulless, as apart from Christianity, the beautiful form was there, into which real life might re-enter. Any thing in society, which is contrary to Christianity, is contrary also to "good manners," unless indeed any society is itself avowedly un-Christian.

The use of the word "world" may also perplex some. "The world" may be used to designate those who "[4] have their portion in this life," for those out of Christ. Yet however miserably large may be the number of those who are going on the broad road, however many may bear the name of Christian without the reality, "[5] the Lord knoweth those who are His;" the Searcher of hearts alone can separate the sheep from the goats. "Some men's sins," the Apostle says[6], "are open beforehand, going before to judgment." From such the Apostle bids us separate ourselves; and it is no good sign, that if men are e. g. notoriously "defilers of their neighbour's wives," such, if they have political influence, or wit, or wealth, or any other secular recommendation, are courted by what is called "the world." But these are few. Even these probably would respect one who avoided intercourse with

[2] 1 Tim. vi. 11.   [3] 2 Tim. ii. 24.
[4] Ps. xvii. 14.   [5] 2 Tim. ii. 19.
[6] 1 Tim. v. 24.

---

them. But the representation in "Modern Christianity" that a consistent Christian (living, it is assumed, in ordinary society) must be hated by all, with whom he comes in contact, assumes an universality of evil. The writer says in his own person;

"[7] I challenge the reader of any Gospel or Epistle in the Scripture, to produce one single page which does not more or less distinctly set forth the truth, that to be hated and persecuted and ridiculed from morning till night by all the world, is, in all ages, ancient and modern alike, the eternal immutable unfailing test of the Christianity that comes from Christ."

"[8] We find it inconvenient to proclaim our religion, wherever we go, to be marked men in every circle wherein we move, to expose ourselves to hatred persecution and ridicule, whenever we come in contact with our neighbours."

The language implies that there is nothing which is not un-Christian and inimical to Christianity, and that we are the judges who are His and who not. Yet this, or the assumption of inconceivable "human respect" which would be ashamed of Christ and His words, lies as the basis of many of those contrasts, that a Christian must either separate himself from all intercourse with his fellow men, or be hated by them.

"[9] While I see them (priests) smiling politely on sin, and caressed by those who would have spat on our Lord."

It belongs to the fiction to make the defender of "Modern Christianity" argue in a very common-place way. The theory is, that the parson, who enters society, dismisses all thought of both his Baptismal and Ordination vows, or thinks every sort of self-indulgence which does not flagrantly contradict both, compatible with both. On his own part, as the assailant, his idea of teaching seems to be that of a thunder or a hailstorm, and he certainly has not had present to his mind Moses' description "[1] my speech doth distil as the dew" or the "[2] here a little and there a little" of Isaiah. I should have thought that Clergy who might feel it to be a duty to go into society, would, with a little

[7] Pref: p. 8.   [8] Ib. p. 9.   [9] p. 140.
[1] Deut. xxxii. 2.   [2] Is. xxviii. 19.

wisdom, have found no difficulty to sow seed at least in the
hearts of individuals, to which God might " [3] give the in-
crease." I do not remember the difficulty.

Christianity has a great task before it, to make " [4] the
kingdoms of this world the kingdoms of our Lord and of
His Christ : " but it is not because they are civilised, but
because, retaining an outward civilisation, they are fast
decaying and becoming uncivilised. Class is being arrayed against class, interest against interest; " union " is becoming fast a name for disunion and antagonism; the
older of us have observed, for well-nigh forty years, the
materials of a worse revolution than that of 1793 : yet
Christianity has not " [5] to fight tooth and nail with civilisation," but by the grace of God to ensoul it.

The anonymous writer dwells much and often on the
evils caused by worldly clergy. I had hoped that this
generation had passed away. I have not met with them.
Only we need not be worldly, because a proportion of us
has been well-endowed ; nor need we "make ourselves
ridiculous " in order, by God's grace, to convert the world.
The world respects those who are consistent and act
on principle, even while they speak against it. In days
relatively cold, Bp. Porteus remonstrated separately with
three ladies of highest rank for the fashionable Sunday re-
ceptions which they held weekly. All listened to him,
though one only permanently abandoned them. Yet he
was respected, not ridiculed, for his remonstrance. We
have people's consciences with us, whether they hear or
whether they forbear. As for our incomes, the question
for our own souls is, not what we have, but what we
do with it. It was said of a Bishop of London, before
the income of his see was reduced, that he "could not
afford" to become Archbishop of Canterbury, because so
much of his income had been appropriated to works for
God, in part for his poorer Clergy.

Christianity has a side, which gains respect from those

[3] 1 Cor. iii. 6.   [4] Rev. xi. 15.   [5] p. 69.

who are not themselves Christians. People admire what
they do not follow. The new commandment is, that ye
" love one another, as I have loved you," with a self-
sacrificing love. And this, whatever political economists
may say, or however people may under false principles
excuse themselves from giving to the poor, the world will
appreciate. Indeed, it has often seemed strange to me
how, even for this world only, the very wealthy so forego
the love of their fellow beings and the happiness of benefitting them and the radiance of their smile of thankfulness,
and can waste on dogs and horses or vanities of the world
what might make them be, and be counted among the
world's benefactors. I have thought that God allowed
them to blind themselves, not willing that great things
should be done to any end, except to His Glory. It would,
for the wealthy, be a cheap way of gaining popularity. But
any how obedience to the Gospel does make people popular.
S. Anthony, the very ideal of an ascetic life and its great
promoter, we are told by his biographer, when young,
" made all to take delight in him." At this moment, one
of the most popular names in England is that of one who
gave very largely, in the hopes of improving the dwellings
of the poor, the late Mr. Peabody. The most popular living
Nobleman, probably, is one of the so-called Evangelical
school, who has associated, not his name only, but himself
with all sorts of works of piety and charity, and especially in benefitting the poor, but has also acted con-
spicuously in the state of life to which it pleased God to
call him, his hereditary position as one of our Lawgivers,
—Lord Shaftesbury. Of course there is the other side
also. Some who hate religion, or strictness, or the Church,
will ridicule, call names, slander, nay persecute, till they
have tested a person's perseverance. But *then*, they will
turn and respect a man the more, because he held on. The
times of open persecution are not yet.

Having mentioned these imperfections in "Modern Christianity &c." it would be wrong not to say, that (personalities

E

and exaggerations [1] apart) the anonymous writer has been
carrying on the same war against worldliness, of which the
terrible revolution of 1793 blew the first trumpet notes;
which was carried on by all earnest men, but perhaps
especially first by the pious Evangelicals; and then, simul-
taneously with them but by a distinct action, by the
Tractarians. He himself indeed accuses the Tractarians
of having [2], "as if out of pure perversity and spite per-
mitted [3] their disciples to indulge in an almost unlimited
amount of secularity." Whence he can have obtained this
impression, I know not. I should have thought that if he
read any of the writings of the Tractarians, he could not
have said it. The old allegation against us was the very
contrary, that we were too strict. I should have thought
that our objection was, that the sphere of worldliness condemned by the Evangelicals was too limited. However,
his own positive pictures of what a Christian ought to be,
and his statement of the witness borne by the prayers
provided for us by the Church of England, are valuable
and true. The penitential character of our Prayer-book
was drawn out some 36 years ago by Isaac Williams, in a
thoughtful essay in the Tracts for the times.

The standard is high, but has, I trust, been in the way
of being realized by many, of whom the world knows
nothing.

"[4] Without immediate reference to Christ, as to a personal guide
standing by, no action is to be performed, no word spoken, no thought
conceived."

Translated into the old language, this is, "Live con-

---

[1] e. g. "Christianity cannot exist in the empire of the intellect and the region of
human prosperity, because it came on purpose to destroy them both," (rather "to
sanctify both.") p. 46. Elsewhere however he says, "There is a variety of secular
pursuits available," and reproaches us for our ignorance of natural history. pp.
130, 131. His bête noire is the richer endowments of the Bishops and of a portion of
the clergy.   [2] p. 29.

[3] I suppose that by "permission" he means the maxims of their school, as expressed
by their writings. And yet he says not of them only, but of the Clergy generally,
" Your preaching is plain enough, and your Sunday standard of Christian holiness all
that can be desired." p. 64.   [4] p. 23.

stantly in the presence of God," and "pray without ceasing."

"[5] He wants your life, and the life of every creature for whom He died, to be given up without reserve to Him."

In the Apostle's words, "Do all in the Name of the Lord Jesus."

"[6] Christ was now to produce a form of testimony altogether new, a testimony real, ever present, personal, a testimony which should proclaim the truth as plainly in modern Paris or London or Berlin as in Jerusalem or Galilee of old. His Spirit must linger here; it must be manifesting Him with a brightness which cannot be hid, wherever His servants and children dwell."

In our Lord's words, "Let your light so shine before men, that they may see your good works and glorify your Father which is in heaven."

Thoughts such as these can never be misplaced, and I hope that they may, by God's grace, find entrance among those whom, without the condiment in which they are enveloped, we could not have reached. I should be glad to think that they would reach some of the worldly, whom they are apparently intended to rouse, and occasion them to review their own standard by the measure of Christ. Unhappily such books mostly fall into the hands of those who amuse themselves with the inconsistencies of others, rather than correct their own. The anonymous writer will forgive the expression of the hope that he will be found in the Great Day to have acted up to the standard, which he lays down; for it is an awful thing to judge others, if we bear in memory our Lord's words[7], "With what judgement ye judge, ye shall be judged; and with what measure ye mete, it shall be measured unto you again."

[5] p. 27.   [6] p. 55, 56.   [7] S. Matt. vii. 2.

PRINTED BY THE SOCIETY OF THE HOLY TRINITY,
HOLY ROOD, OXFORD.

www.ingramcontent.com/pod-product-compliance
Lightning Source LLC
Chambersburg PA
CBHW021441090426
42739CB00009B/1589